To Elizabeth Colson who knew all of them

Ursula Gröhn-Wittern

A Large Dam, Small Fish and the BaTonga

95 years of Zambian History observed by Gray K. Madyenkuku

www.tredition.de

© 2017 Ursula Gröhn-Wittern

Verlag: tredition GmbH, Hamburg

ISBN
Paperback: 978-3-7345-5523-7
Hardcover: 978-3-7345-5524-4
e-Book: 978-3-7345-5525-1

Printed in Germany

I tell you, whenever you did this for one of the least important of these brothers of mine, you did it for me.

Matthew 25, 40

Photos:

Front cover: The river god Nyaminyami [i,] Kariba [ii] Dam, Kapenta Fishing rigs, Tonga Girl

Back cover: Gray Madyenkuku and author 2016

Map on page is by Gossner Mission

Layout cover: Druckerei St. Pauli, Hamburg

Introduction

In 1984 I started to work on a three- year contract as an agricultural adviser for a seed multiplication and distribution programme in the former Gwembe South Development Project (GSDP) in Southern Province of Zambia. BaGray, as he is called by his friends, became my source of knowledge and advice in many ways.

This book is the tribute I pay to his patience, knowledge and friendship. I feel a great need to preserve the voices of people who have seen such a long time of social, economic and political change in a country like Zambia as he has.

BaGray was 95 years old when my husband and I spent a week together with him at his home near Sinazongwe in 2016, recording his memories but also discussing many topics ranging from the Brexit (happening at that time), to birth control and the problems of an ageing population in Germany, to the upcoming elections in Zambia or the pollution of rivers and air by the mining industry.

I do not agree with all of his views but respect his conclusions as a result of the observations he made and his deep belief in the words of the Bible. I have tried to keep to his wording as close as possible. Some things though, need explanations for the reader who is not familiar with certain events and terms. This is done in the footnotes I added.

Father of 33 living children and numerous grandchildren and greatgrandchildren he is spending his days at home, keenly interested in the world and at the same time humbly thanking God for every day He gives and the food on his table.

The people of Zambia are close to me and my husband. We hope this can be a small contribution and a sign of the love and respect we feel for all those who really try to contribute to a peaceful and just development without pursuing their personal advantage.

I would like to thank Gossner Mission for the support in Lusaka and the work done by the staff of the Kaluli Development Foundation especially Mr. Milupi Silumesii at Nkandabbwe, Sinazongwe district.

Ursula Gröhn-Wittern

August, 2016

Some of the original recordings can be accessed through the QR Codes in the book.

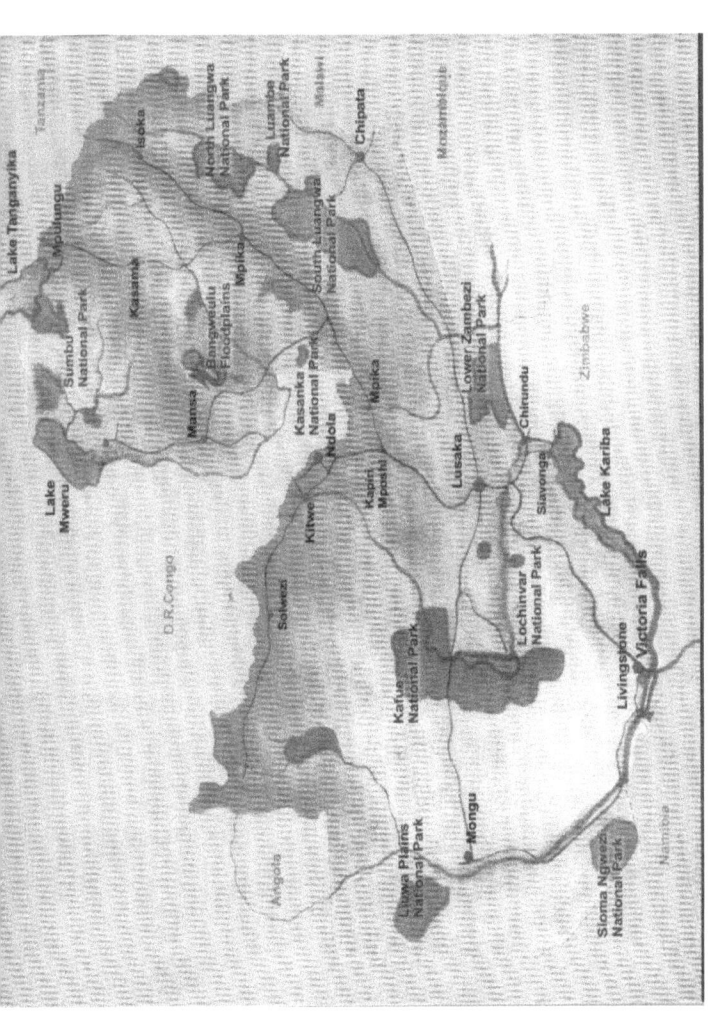

9

Gray Kanini Madyenkuku

Gray Kanini Madyenkuku

My name is Gray Kanini Madyenkuku. I was born in Siameja in the Gwembe District, Zambia on the March 3 in 1921.

My father was a teacher-evangelist. He was a class teacher running an elementary school. He first opened a new school in Sinakasikili in 1923. There we stayed up to 1927 when we shifted to open another school in Mweemba´s area. We stayed there for three years and were transferred to go across from Northern Rhodesia to Southern Rhodesia to open a school in the village of Binga.

That is where I started learning and grew up. In 1926, my brother, the son of my aunt, took me to Kabanga Mission where I had to go into Tonga primary part two. Within the same year, I went into English reader one. When I came back for holidays, the missionary at Kanchindu blamed my father for sending me to another people´s denomination to get my education. So I didn't go back to Kabanga Mission which was catholic. I remained at Kanchindu Methodist Mission where I had to start with standard one.

In 1926 the provincial education officer, Mr. Bell from Livingstone came and after testing class standard one, I was one of three boys who were transferred straight away into standard three.

The point made by him was, that one should not waste people's time when they already know everything.

I went on with Kanchindu Mission. That same year we transferred the whole mission to go to Masuku Mission because the white missionaries did not like the heat of the Gwembe Valley. So they had to go to a cooler place. Masuku Mission at that time was built in the land of the senior headman Siasikabole in Singani chiefdom.

While there, I was put into standard four and at the end of 1928 I went to Kafue Mission for standard five and six.

In 1931 I was supposed to go to the Secondary school in Munali but the missionaries discouraged me as well as my father. They said that I should not go because I was still too young.

So, I requested them that I should go to the medical school. In September I got my chance to become one of the students of the third class of Lusaka Medical School. After two and a half years I qualified as a medical assistant.

In 1933 I was posted to Abercorn (now called Mbala), Northern Province where I worked as a responsible person in the wards. My job was in the outpatient department.

In the absence for the man who was working in the pathological laboratory I had to take over. So

I found my place to my ability and the medical officer, Dr Sutherland at that time, talked to the senior men and the sister in charge to let me act as I felt to any patient in his absence.

When a new patient had to be admitted, I was consulted by these senior men. Looking at my age, they did not like that. But what could they do? The medical officer had given instruction and they had to follow.

In 1946 I got married to a lady from home. 1948 I was transferred to Kanchindu Methodist Mission dispensary on the banks of the Zambesi River in Chief Mweemba area, earlier Mododoli Community. All of this was before the resettlement[iii] and giving way to the construction of Lake Kariba.

Church at Kanchindu, built after resettlement

In 1951 I was called to Choma Hospital for a re-fresher course. 1953 I left the job because I had to come home after the death of my father to take care of my old mother.

1954 I left Mweemba area for Sinazongwe where I opened up a small shop at Siamajele village. I lived on farming and when the Kariba dam came, I lived both on farming and fishing. 1955 I was elected as a member of Gwembe Native Author-ity for Sinazongwe Chieftaincy.

1956, as a consequence of the resettlement, we

shifted to Nkandabbwe with all the villages around, to give way to the construction of Kariba Dam.

After independence in 1964 I lived on fishing and agriculture. But in the year 1970, when a group of the Gossner[iv] Service Team came, I was employed to help them settle and continue work among the people in Gwembe South (now Sinazongwe district). My activities were being a secretary of the project and representative at the council meetings and in other meetings in the villages with the people where ever we had to open an activity.

In this programme, I worked in the Siatwinda Irrigation scheme and we made some extension at Kafwambila on small scale irrigation with hand pumps. We had a few farmers who were given hand pumps for irrigation and were growing maize, tomatoes, cabbage and rice.

In Kafwambila it was an eye-opening experience to the people to see that they could do something of this kind by themselves without spending a lot of money. The only money that would be spent would be on the hand pump and a few metres of piping and then the water would be running to the field through a canal. This was easy to understand and they made it a good practice although they were very far away from the line of rail and very few visitors came. But among themselves they made business.

At Siameja we organized a shop as a cooperative for the locals and it was doing well. We were selling mealie meal, maize, sugar and so on. It was the second shop in the area. Mr. Sikuzeka was running the other shop but the cooperative shop that was run under the organisation of the GSDP (Gwembe South Development Project) [v] did much better. But unfortunately, all this collapsed after the departure of the GSDP team in 1998.

During the famines we took a lot of help and delivered maize to the villages and the hungry.

I was organising the deliveries here and there. Every time we had meetings I was always the secretary.

That was my duty and apart from these I was the chairman of the Sinazeze Agricultural Society and I was a representative of the GSDP at the council meetings and the secretary of the Gwembe District Agricultural Shows.

I took an active part at the provincial show collecting the items which were taken to the show from Sinazongwe and often I was the interpreter.

I worked with the GSDP project from 1970 to

1988. Then I stopped. In between I was a member of the SPCMU (Southern Province Corporate Marketing Union) which was located in Choma. Every time SPCMU had meetings I was a member representing Sinazongwe Society. I was a member for six years and during that time I was acting chairman of Fisheries Organisation which represented the fishermen of Sinazongwe area and at times we had to go with the secretary of the fishermen to deal with the matters in the meetings of fisheries. One time we went to Kitwe and very often we had these meetings in the Gwembe Valley.

Most of my life I spent as an active person in various committees. I have been secretary or chairman in one of the school meetings, too.

And at my home I remained a farmer and a leading farmer so far. For two successive Gwembe shows at Munyumbwe I have won gifts. The first gift was a scotch cart and then a ridge plow.

Up to now I have four wives and a number of children and grandchildren.

My first wife and I had 12 children but we are remaining with six. All six are busy and free to live on their own. They are active people. One of them once was a Member of Parliament for the Movement for Multi-party Democracy (MMD) party.

The youngest and the oldest

One is teacher leading a school in Lusaka, one works for an electric company in Kalomo, some of them are teachers.

With the second wife, I have four male children and five females alive and one left us.

Some of those who left us left us grandchildren. We are taking them to school. Some have finished their education and are working. One is a male nurse and one just finished his diploma in administrative work.

Of the four boys of my second wife, two are trading and farming.

Of the five girls one is a teacher, one a nurse and one just finished as a pharmacist, yet to be employed. The other two live on their own on small scale farming.

With my third wife, I have eight living children. Two have left us very young. The living ones live as traders. One of the boys is a pastor in Lusaka.

I have 10 living children with my fourth wife. The last one was a stillborn. They are workers, one a veterinary assistant, one working for the health department; three are still in training and education. One is in grade 12 and one in grade 8.

So, we are living very active lives and we are working hard trying to make our children strong enough to make their life easy.

We are a church-going family. Except for one none of our children drinks beer. All of them are found in churches.

Part of the Madyenkuku family in June 2016

Trip to Germany and USA

In the year 1982 I was on a visit to Germany on invitation of Gossner Mission to learn how people live and work and seeing the general atmosphere in Germany. We first arrived in Berlin at the setting of the sun and were taken to the house of the first Gossner team leader who opened Siatwiinda Irrigation Scheme. We spent two days with his family and visited places they thought we should see. We went to a place near the German university which was opened by Martin Luther.

After two days, we had to cross the Berlin Wall to Eastern Germany. And here we were received by a missionary, a member of Gossner Mission and were taken right into the villages. They call it villages although they are small towns. There, they do a lot of farming and we spend two days there.

We were travelling through their farms looking at the management. They were very active growing Irish potatoes, which is the main food there. They make sugar out of sugar beet not sugar cane. We went to a sugar plant. I was with my friend Mr. Chiwena the Provincial Agricultural Officer in Choma at that time. He had been in America for training. It was easy for us to understand what was going on. We spent almost one month there and returned happily and full of ideas.

If we made use of the land as our friends there do, we would have no problems. A small piece of land gains them an income. While we have bigger land we have little harvest. We need to improve.

My second trip overseas was to America, I was invited by an organisation dealing with national dams. Some of them small compared to Kariba dam. We landed in London and flew to Baltimore and stayed in Maryland for a week attending a meeting on River Basin development. The main subject was on how we should go about such big dams as Kariba. This was introduced by Mr. Thyer Scudder. Because it was found that these operations cause a lot of problems for the people. Some participants came from North Africa and Israel. We discussed how to improve the way we treat people who have to be removed when a dam is built. Not just to give them a little because they do not know any better.

Who gets the most profit? What care do they need and how long? It is a problem where ever such dams are constructed. The result was that one must take care before such a construction takes place. The project here was organised by Mr. Scudder and Mrs. Colson[vi].

Independence of Zambia

The struggle for independence of the people of Northern Rhodesia affected the Gwembe Valley and the whole territory.

Starting from 1940 there was a shakeup in the country. People could act independently in many ways.

I remember one day in Lusaka, I went to the butcher with a Lozi friend, Mr Munalula. We came to the door and only to be told to go to the window[vii]. At the window, we were asked what we wanted. Mr. Munalula demanded a head of a cow. Now, the salesman persisted we must go to the door. Then we left without going to the door, because at the beginning we were told to go to the window. Therefore, let the head of the cow be brought to us through the window and as that was not possible, we left.

Another time I went into a shop alone and as I came to the door I was told to go to the window. When I got there, I was asked what I wanted and I said that I wanted to buy a bed.

Then, I was told to go to the door but I said I wanted the bed be brought through the window because when I was at the door, they told me to go to the window without asking me what I wanted. As the bed could not be pushed through the window I left. The manager blamed the sales-person badly for not taking interest of the custom-ers. But I left although the manager tried to call me back to the door.

One day, Mr Munalula and I went to a private doctor in Lusaka. He let us in and I lead my friend as if he was a sick person. We were given a seat and the doctor went and came back with syringe with something in it and ordered me to strip my patient for the injection. I asked him what was in the syringe, since he had not asked him what he suffered from. How did he know before knowing what the patient´s complaint was? He persisted that the man must be given an injection. My friend screamed and we left.

And my friend continued to walk as if he was very sick and we said loudly: "Let us go to the hospital where we will be helped". We made it a joke.

So, a lot of funny things were exercised during this period to tease the white man who did not want the Africans to get into their shops and be served by the door. At the day of independence this ended.

When independence was acquired, all was in the hands of the citizens. It was a mixture of good and bad. It shortly got better in some ways. The main problem at that moment was economic, which went up and down. That was the problem we had to struggle with and think of means of how we could have a stable economy.

Independence of our country Zambia was born on 24th of June, 1964.

Before independence we had problems with

health facilities in Sinazongwe District and all districts. But after independence we were able to fight for health units. We had very few of them and they were not as helpful as the communities would have liked because they were far apart from each other. And for patients to walk to the clinics was a big problem. Everything meant walking and it was difficult to carry patients. But after independence our government built clinics closer by, here and there in walking distance and the distance you had to carry a patient diminished.

We have a hospital in Maamba now that gets patients from all over the area. There is even some transport and there are many more transport facilities these days because many of our children are buying motor vehicles. When you go to Sinazeze today, you find a lot of vehicles parked there. Some are passing through on business of buying fish or cotton. And some are transporting people. At daybreak, they are there on the road. Travelling is easy now.

Then, it was difficult to find a store to buy salt or sugar or whatever. You had to go far, even to the line of rail. But now there are shops belonging to our boys where we can get these things. That is development.

View of Lake Kariba

We thank God for independence and that we can do as we like as long as we keep to the law. There is no disadvantage of independence. What I cry for now is peace.

Zambia has been a peaceful country since independence and I desire that Zambia remains peaceful as other countries have been. Therefore, I plead to the politicians that they should not cause fighting and throwing of stones over this and that. We don´t want this type of fight. We want peace.

Suppose you die because of such a fight, what

do you gain? Let us go to the polls peacefully.

Let us accept the result as was the case from the beginning. No war, no quarrelling, peace, peace, peace!

I therefore request those who vote to go to vote freely without quarrelling. Those, who have ideas of anarchy, should refrain from that. Because fighting does not pay, it only destroys.[viii]

The days of the Zambezi River

Before the construction of the Kariba dam people
over the Gwembe Valley lived on small-scale agriculture. They had no support from anybody.
They had to run their own fields. The main crops
were finger millet and maila[ix] and small crops like
pumpkins and others. These crops were grown
during the rainy season. Some were also grown
in Zilili gardens, after the rainy season in the river
basin of the Zambesi. The river inundated its

banks, people made gardens when the water receded, growing maize and pumpkins an and when the water receded, growing of maize and pumpkins commenced.

In case of famine those who had zilili gardens had no problem. Even when the rains were poor, they could get a little from the garden.

There, they also had the chance to fish with fishing baskets made of small sticks. These were laid in the water and lifted out to get the fish. Some people also used metallic hooks.

They also constructed a wall of reeds across the river and trapped the fish behind it.

With the new times of the dam and independence, people changed to the big fishing systems and the government introduced the growing of cotton and sunflower and extended the growing of maize.

However, during the old days people were living happily, because they could go hunting in the forest. There were no rules stopping them. They could hunt small animals up to a buffalo. They could also look for fruit from the bush. A lot of amenities were good and free from the bush but are now under control of the government. No hunting can be done, everything is under the officers. The freedom that people had is strictly gone. What remains now is to follow whatever government advises the people to do. It is a big challenge for the elderly people.

But the elderly people are finishing. Only a few are still there. Those who remain do not know the days of the Zambesi River. They only know the lake and do not miss anything. But we, the old people, miss something.

How education came

Education started when the missionaries arrived from wherever they came from, particularly from Europe. As there were no educated people here, they came with people from those areas where they had taught before. For example: When they came to Northern Rhodesia they brought with them people from South Africa who were teachers.

At Kanchindu, the first school of the Methodist

church in Northern Rhodesia, there were teachers who were Basutu (from a country now called Lesotho).

My father was one of the first boys to be recruited at Kanchindu Mission under the leadership of Reverend fellow of the Methodist Church. The group of which my father was one, was taught how to write Tonga, how to do arithmetics and anything of the ideas the white man brought with him. The students were taught in various ways.

The teachers of that time when teaching they had to do everything. If one was sent to a certain place as a teacher one was able to do everything; like building, carpentry, planting of crops, planting of trees and so on. This man was a jack- of-all-trades. He did not go there only to teach the ABC. No. He came with everything the white man had come with from Europe. The building of a school at the place where he was sent to was no problem for him. He could do the agricultural, do the building of the house and so on. He could do it because he was taught.

People went from smaller schools like Kanchindu for larger schools like Kafue which was the highest school of the Methodist Church for men. For women, it was Chipembi Mission (now in Chibombo district). These two schools were to teach the skills of the new civilization. Not as it is done now. Most school boys are just taught from books but they cannot extend their knowledge to other fields. They cannot do building, carpentry and so on. They must acquire these skills at different places. While at that time, they learnt the skill at school.

The teachers of those days were busy people. Teachers of today are busy with book work but not hand work.

The teachers at that time were preachers as well as evangelists. They had the duty to go and preach every Saturday and Sunday in the villages, preaching the gospel of the Bible. Teachers nowadays are so free that they can go to the beer hall or do whatever pleases them.

But at that time a teacher was not as a free as that. Because, on weekdays he was teaching the class, on Saturday and Sunday, this man, according to his denomination, was busy going to the villagers preaching the gospel. So today, you'll find a teacher has nothing to do with the Gospel, except for a few cases but not normally.

You may wonder how my father got to Kanchindu School. One day a missionary came to the villages and it happened that he was preaching in Siameja Village. My father as a young boy was listening.

Typical landscape of Sinazongwe district

After the preaching, the preacher, a white man, told my father and other boys to come with him to Kanchindu Mission which was six miles away. The boys were recruited with fear of the white man but they were interested in how they would be treated and what they could learn. When they came back to the village because they missed their parents, they felt good and then many others followed.

That is how education came in the country, particularly to the Gwembe Valley. Missionaries were building new schools here and there in the villages, sending the boys from Kanchindu to Kafue and from Kafue they were sent back in the villages as teachers.

The ending of their education was Standard Two. As long as they were able to read Tonga fluently, they were qualified enough to come back as teachers. Gradually it went on.

We children, particularly I and my brothers, the sons of my father, found ourselves trapped in a net. I cannot beat the Budima drums or blow the horns like the boys that grew up in the village, because I was kept under control. The missionaries viewed the Budima and dances as pagan and told us not to join those games. But funny enough, they went there to watch but refused to act.

That is how it was everywhere where schools of any denomination were opened. Their character influenced the new society for example the character of the Adventist Church or the Methodist Church. As a result, the Adventists and the Sunday people are not united as they should be. They look at each other differently. This has spoiled their attitude

Traditional Tonga homestead in 1986

Health and Education after

Independence

We had very few primary schools dotted around
our territory. After independence, these were in-
creased tremendously and up to now they are in-
creasing. This is a very big development. We did
not have a university, but there it is now! And
there are many other colleges dotted around the
country.

So, on the side of education, we acquired what we would not have acquired if we were not independent. Because the colonial and the federal government did not give much attention to the education of the black man. So far I could say.

On the health side, too, we have so many health centres and hospitals after independence. We even have the University Teaching Hospital which is advanced compared to the first medical school. That is an achievement on a high level. Concerning the complaints now in connection with the hospitals it is the lack of feeding facilities[x] at some times in some large hospitals in the rural areas and at times shortages of medicines. However, we have some transport facilities now, although not enough, taking patients from home to the clinics and from the clinics to the hospitals, like Maamba.

We still need more facilities in both education and health.

Therefore, as we will go to the polls soon, we expect God, the creator, to lead to find the right person ready enough to continue in bringing us more education and health and rural development.

Infrastructure is highly required. The improvement of roads and opening up new roads is worthwhile. So, we are looking forward to seeing

a difference between the colonial or federal government and our black government.

I believe the struggle has not ended. It is still going on until all the shortages of commodities and
high prices which make life hard are tackled and
until everything is smooth.

Young people dancing in 1986

Traditions

In the olden days in the Gwembe Valley the Budima[xi] dance was a very famous game but it was
not something that could be done at any time. It
was only done when mourning during the funerals. Of course, at the funeral of a small baby it
was not necessary to drum up the Budima. But
for a reasonable grown-up person it was done.
And it was much more for people who were big

enough and famous enough that many drummers from other villages would come to that village to do the mourning. Up to 10 groups or so would come to do the drumming and blow the horns. Those, who did the dancing could make the meaning of the horns clear to the listeners.

When the budima was sounded ten miles away, People far away knew that there was a funeral and that somebody had died. Depending on how many drums would sound, people could distinguish whether the person who had died was a famous man, because for an unimportant man the sound would be less.

They were knowledgeable to translate the meaning of the horns and drums. Drums of seven sizes from small to very big were used. The groups carried the heavy drums on their shoulders eagerly without tiring. The sound of the drums would reach even villages located within a reasonable distance.

After the building of the dam this became a thing that was done at other occasions than funerals, too.

Drummers were requested to drum at the independence grounds. And that is how it is done now. But unfortunately, this drumming too is dying out. Very rarely do you hear them nowadays and there are very few areas where they are still being drummed. We call it civilization but it makes us loose this famous system (of our cultural identity).

Is it good? We elderly call it a loss but for those who did not know the old style and who were born during independence and after, do not have the desire to hear the sound when there is a funeral. Sooner or later it will be heard no more.

This custom is dying. Should it be saved? We want to keep the culture of this country but are we not losing it at the same time?

Another thing that is lost is a dance that was done by youngsters.

It has nothing to do with funerals. In the evening after the meal in each village the Kalilo or ching'ande dance was done. This has died. So, our culture is disappearing one by one. What does the community do about this? They do not value this because at its best they were not there. Is this not diminishing the history of the country, the history of that locality?

Today`s civilisation is causing things to diminish. What do people run after now? TV and other scientific developments taking place. You find children instead of picking up a book to read, they are just gazing at the TV.

They see people playing around, doing things that are not wanted for the young to be seen. Young boys are looking at videos with what we call tondwa[xii]. There is no "tondwa" anymore. Is that civilization in the right way? To be exposed to such things?

So, we see, we are losing what we knew. How do we keep nature going if some things are lost and some things are exposing taboos?

I give you a thought to think about: The youngsters nowadays watch people go to bed with married women on TV. Is that necessary? We are killing nature and it does not go well with the Gospel.

I am talking to the leaders: Can you do something about it that such things are not exposed to the children? What are we doing? Where are we going?

What has taken over is Christianity with so many different denominations.

The training people are getting from the word of God has caused that these traditions like Budima and Kalilo collapse. However, when we look at the value, we find that the value of Christian influence is much better than the older traditions.

If one understands that, then he is comforted. It is better to have the Christian way of life through the churches than the old type of life that we lived.

Fishing

The fishing which was not there before and which came because of Kariba Dam has caused the people who decided to practice fishing to get money. With this money, they were able to buy what they needed, like clothing, good food or sending children to school. It even changed the style of the houses.

Even with the little money a man would get, he will use it to protect himself by buying clothes, by buying corrugated iron for the roof of his small hut. The huts now are no longer built of mud and sticks and grass but of burned bricks and this is an advantage.

This development has come about because of gains from fishery and at the same time the improvement of agriculture by growing sunflower and other crops that can be sold like vegetables and fruit. They can be obtained because of the opening of roads. People travel up and down from one point to the other. And the local people may collect some fruit from the bush and sell it at the roadside for the travelers to buy.

This brings some income and clothing in skins and fibres is no longer practiced. Everyone wears cloth. People buy either second hand clothes from overseas or new clothes which traders bring to the Gwembe Valley in exchange for fish.

When the system of Kapenta[xiii] fishing was introduced, only the rich people, the white people, managed to get rigs to fish Kapenta. They monopolised the business for quite some time, without the local people participating. The local people were only employed by these Kapenta fishers. But eventually, the local people, our young men, went into fishing and multiplied the number of rigs, especially for the last five years and it has become very big business on the side of the local people.

Now, as the local people went on multiplying and putting more rigs on the lake, the white men have left Kapenta fishing unconditionally. I cannot say why. But there remain a few who are rearing crocodiles now. I do not know what they do with them. But they value the skins of the crocodiles. Some people are enjoying the meat of the crocodiles now. I also hear that the crocodile keepers transport the meat to other countries.

This is part of the value from the lake. I don't know whether sooner or later also the local young man will begin to go into crocodile keeping. They may.

There seems to be a competition between Kapenta fishing and the ordinary fishing with nets where you catch breams (oreochromis niloticus), Bottlenose (*Mormyrus longirostris*), tiger fish (*Hydrocynus vittatus*) and Cornish Jack (*Mormyrops anguilloides).*

Before Kariba dam the Zambesi had no Kapenta fish. They were introduced from the lakes of the northern parts of Zambia. They were put in by the Department of Fisheries and started breeding there. Then fishing was allowed.

Here in Sinazongwe we are thankful that this development has come.

Baobab trees are typical for the Zambesi valley

Development

In 1970 the government brought in a team of the
Gossner Mission which settled at Nkandabwe
and opened an irrigation scheme at Siatwiinda.
They came specifically for irrigation development
and although Siatwiinda irrigation is not used at
the moment because the lake has receded
greatly making water scarce, the knowledge of
growing things by watering is carried by the people. They make gardens wherever there is water

nearby and there they produce vegetables and maize. And these crops feed the families. The extend of famine is very mild these years. Not only at Siatwiinda but the extension of this education went as far as Kafwambila where hand pumps are used. People learnt what to do when you do not have the proper technology at hand. So they use bucket irrigation and so on and this can help them.

People have learnt a lot and gained a lot. The new generation which does not know the time and the places that are under water now, take it that it was always like this.

That is development and we must thank for that.

The Gossner Service Team (GST) came to run the irrigation schemes at Siatwiinda and Buleya Malima and enlarged them. Buleya Malima was started by the Ministry of Agriculture and was then handed over to Gossner Mission. During that time it was run by the Ministry and the local people were not participating as it was a government project. When the GST took over there was an arrangement with the government to open up new land for the people to participate. It did not take long for them to learn because they had already learnt while they were employed by the government. It was nice and progressive and good business because many people from the line of rail came to buy the product of vegetable and fruits (citrus). Now there is a disturbance, because the lake waters have receded too far and as such the irrigation scheme pumps cannot get the water on the land. Therefore, the prosperity of that time is dwindling. Let us hope some success is made in an event that the water can come back.

It is the same at Siatwiinda. People there had adopted the system of irrigation very well and had customers buying tomatoes and all sorts of vegetables. They were even growing rice at a large scale. These two projects are not as active now as they were before.

But these programmes had a very good influence because people are working with buckets now, growing tomatoes and impwa. The influence of Gossner Mission is still going on but the standard of hope that was there when the water was up, is no longer there and this is a setback. Let us hope this will improve.

The GST had a lot of activities. They encouraged the people to work in groups making bricks. That was useful because they found customers. The people were interested in buying bricks and learnt from the cooperative to make their own bricks.

The Tonga crafts^{xiv} project had taken off tremendously but now, since the departure of the GST, it is a thing of the past.

There were many things that were tried by them but because of no interest of the Department of Agriculture that has taken over, the practical things were forgotten. We encourage the government to look into this. People learnt the growing of cotton but after the death of the cooperative movement the growing of cotton went down because LINTCO^{xv} stopped.

People need active incentives from the government. Therefore, the government should strengthen the cooperative movement.

People had to move to Muziyo village in the mountains

Buchi means Honey

Let us now talk about the GVDC which is Gwembe Valley Development Company, locally called "buchi". Buchi came about emphasising that this company has brought something sweet, like honey. Therefore, we thought of accepting it, when we were addressed about it.

This company came in 1986. The company grew

cotton, cotton, cotton and wheat. When cotton was grown, many people were employed to do weeding and other work. After the wheat, the local people were allowed to go in after the main harvesting and collect what was left on the fields and keep it. That was truly buchi. This went on for three or four years. But all of a sudden, without our knowledge as locals, the company collapsed.

Another company came, which was Gwembe Grain Growers. They grew wheat and sorghum and they too allowed people to collect the remains of the harvest. They too failed. Then came Agriflora. It grew different crops like green corn, flowers for export and green beans. They introduced the system organic agriculture. This company failed, too.

Now we have the fourth company: ZAMBEEF, which is a Zambian company[xvi] that slaughters cattle and buys peoples´ cattle. People have no say on the price. They are just told the price. It would be better if they were involved so that they can go together.

At the moment, the company is doing very well. They do not allow the collection of the maize they grow, instead they simply burn it. So Buchi is no longer sweet.

There is a big complaint about employment. The company`s senior staff are all non-local people.

Only one, an electrician, who remained since the first company is a local man. But in all the other sections, those in senior jobs have come from somewhere. They are non-locals. There is a big cry to enjoy the value of our soil, too.

Locals are only employed as simple labourers, laid off when there is no work. Could it not be possible to train the local people? Get them in permanent employment? Let us hope the district council and those in power will look at this problem. We have given our soil; we must be given the ability also to be participants in full, not others who come from other districts.

People who lived on the land where GVDC was and where ZAMBEEF is now, were made to shift to the mountains between the Valley and the Plateau to a place called Muziyo. And there were promises by GVDC that they would do some development activities. But up to now people have not seen these developments. The GSDP struggled to have a clinic in Muziyo and a school and a dam. These were the only little projects the people did receive. But they continue to have many problems in the area. I feel they should be looked at by relevant authorities. Therefore, I argue that those in power, including the council and the district should see to it that more attention is given to the people at Muziyo who had to leave because of "Buchi".

Let us make it a happy place for those who had to leave for the mountains. They should be looked after. So as the cropping at the companies is done they must be getting something from the companies.

What is ZAMBEEF doing for the people? What did we agree to with the first company? That the roads should not be closed for the people to walk from the lake to the villages. These places are closed now and people have to go around a long way. What happened to these first agreements? Why were they destroyed? So please: The council: Look into this, so that people are taken care of.

Further Reading:

Clements Frank, 1959, Kariba. The Struggle with the River God, Methuen & Co Ltd

Colson Elizabeth,1971, The social Consequences of Resettlement, Kariba Studies, Manchester University Press

Reynolds Barrie, 1968, The material Culture of the Peoples of the Gwembe Valley 1 and 2, Frederick A. Praeger, N.Y.

Reynolds Pamela, 1989, The Tonga Book of the Earth, Panos Books from the South

Scudder Thayer, 1962 The Ecology of the Gwembe Tonga, Kariba Studies IV, Manchester University Press

i   In Tonga tradition, Nyaminyami (a mythical creature with the head of a serpent and the tail of a fish) was a benevolent Spirit, providing for his people in times of drought or flood by offering his flesh for them to eat. However, the building of the Kariba dam angered him and separated him from his wife who became trapped downstream during its construction. He vowed to wreak havoc and destroy the wall one day. He had made several attempts - two major floods during construction in the 1950s succeeded in breaching the coffer dam and setting back progress for many months. However, the Tonga believe that in the end his wrath was overcome and the wall has held back the waters ever since.

ii   The name 'Kariba' is thought to be a corruption of a local word 'Kariva' which means "little trap". It is believed when those who wished to construct the dam wall wanted to explain the nature of the project to the locals, they emphasised that they wanted to build a little water trap-Kariva. However, the complex pronunciation of the 'v' in Kariva saw the Western constructors produce a sound much like a 'b' hence the creation of the word Kariba.

iii   The resettlement of the BaTonga affected some 57.000 people who had to leave their villages and fertile land near the Zambesi for drier and less favourable land higher up. 23.000 went to the Southern Rhodesia side while 34.000 went to the Northern Rhodesia side. They received little compensation, thus those who went to Northern Rhodesia side received a little sum of £5 each, while those on the Southern Rhodesian side none at all. In spite of this traumatic experience it remained peaceful. In a sense the BaTonga can be regarded as one of the first environmental refugees.

iv   Gossner Mission sent staff to the GSPD in a co-operation with the Government of Zambia

v   The Gwembe South Development Project was the joint rural development project by Gossner Mission and the Government of the Republic of Zambia. It was converted into a Zambian NGO called Kaluli Development Foundation (KDF) which is running projects in the area now.

vi   Dr. Elizabeth Colson studied the culture of the Tonga people in depth. She worked at Berkeley University, California. Dr. Thayer Scudder is an expert on the consequences of resettlement, also at Berkeley. She passed away at the age of 99 years in Monze, Zambia in June 2016.

vii   Before Independence black people were not allowed to enter the shops and were served through a window

vii   said in the anticipation of the elections to be held on August 11, 2016.

ix   Maila is a variety of sorghum used for beer brewing and in ritual. It is early maturing.

x   In african hospitals meals must be cooked and provided by the patient´s family

xi   A set of Budima drums consists of seven drums from small to very large. Horns are also blown. For the untrained ear there seems to be no melody or rule. It is a unique and very old music.

xii   Tondwa refers to sex related issues which are taboo for the young.

xiii   Kapenta (*Limnothrissa mioden*) is a small sardine like fish which was introduced from Lake Tanganyika. It is dried in the sun and a very important source of protein

xiv   This project encouraged pottery and basket weaving and other traditional Skills. The products were bought and sold in shops in Lusaka and elsewhere.

xv   From 1977 to 1994, Zambia's cotton sector was organized around the state-owned cotton company LINTCO (Lint Company of Zambia). On behalf of government, LINTCO purchased seed cotton from farmers at a fixed price, provided certified seed, pesticides, sprayers, and bags and provided extension advice to farmers. LINTCO had a near monopoly in buying seed cotton and in distributing cotton inputs on credit.   In 1994, as part of a broad-based effort to restructure Zambia's economy, LINTCO was sold to two private companies, Lonrho Cotton and Clark Cotton

xvi   now British

Gosser Mission is supporting development through the Kaluli Development Foundation. If you want to help the people in Sinazongwe District, you can donate here:

www.gossner-mission.de

Gossner Mission

Evangelische Bank

IBAN DE 35 5206 0410 0003 9014 91

BIC GENODEF1EK1

Georgenkirchstrasse 69-70

10249 Berlin

Information on Zambia

Estimated population	16.212 mio.(2015)
GDP nominal	20.574 billion
Area	291 sq mi/753 km ^{2}
Government	Unitary Presidencial Republic
Legislature	national assembly
Population Groth	3%
Official language	English
Capital	Lusaka

North Western Rhodesia	27 June 1890
North Eastern Rhodesia	29 January 1900

Amalgamation of Northern Rhodesia 17 August 1911

Federation of Rhodesia and Nyasaland   1 August 1953

Republic of Zambia   24 October 1964

Independence from the United Kingdom

Current constitution   5 January 2016

Human Development Index   139 (2014)

Currency   Zambian Kwacha

Zambia Tourist Information: www.zambiatourism.com

Zambian Embassy: www.zambiaembassy.de

Traditional Exports: Copper, Cobalt, Electricity, Tobacco, Cotton, Floriculture/Horticultural products, Gemstones, Timber, Cement and Textiles.

Major Imports: Crude oil, Chemicals, Medicines, Machinery, Iron, Steel, Manufactured goods, Transportation equipment, Fertilizer and Clothing.

Major Economic Activities: Mining, Agriculture, Construction, Energy, Manufacturing and Tourism. (Wikipedia)

Zeitfracht Medien GmbH
Ferdinand-Jühlke-Straße 7
99095 Erfurt, Deutschland
produktsicherheit@kolibri360.de